GEORGE MICHAEL

FREEDOM

THE ULTIMATE TRIBUTE 1963-2016

David Nolan is an award-winning author and documentary maker. He's written biographies on The 1975, Ed Sheeran, Damon Albarn and Tony Wilson.

THIS IS A CARLTON BOOK

Published by Carlton Books Ltd
20 Mortimer Street
London W1T 3JW

Text and design © 2017 Carlton Books Ltd

ISBN 978-1-78097-979-3

Editor: Chris Mitchell and Victoria Marshallsay
Design: Russell Knowles and Emma Wicks
Production: Lisa Hedicker
Picture Research: Steve Behan

A CIP catalogue for this book is available from the British Library

Printed in Dubai

10 9 8 7 6 5 4 3

GEORGE MICHAEL

FREEDOM

THE ULTIMATE TRIBUTE 1963-2016

DAVID NOLAN

CARLTON
BOOKS

CONTENTS

LEFT George Michael performing in Rotterdam in 1988.

HARD TIMES CHEEK

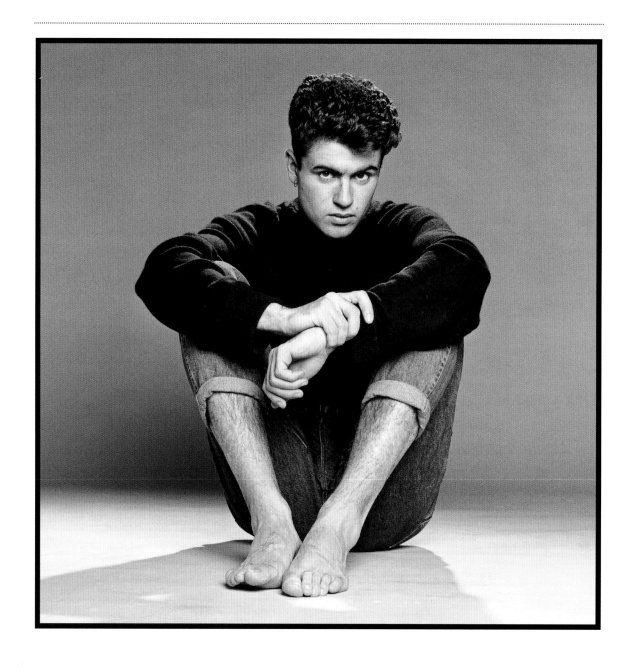

When it came to providing "water-cooler moments" – at a time before most people in Britain even knew what a water cooler was – then BBC TV show *Top of the Pops* was always the best place to find them. Thursday night was the place to receive your weekly supply of pop culture ammunition for everything that would be worth discussing in the playground or works' canteen the following day. And, depending on your age, there would be key moments in the show's history that would define generations.

For the seventies glam rockers, it was David Bowie performing "Starman" in July 1972. For the indie crowd, The Smiths and "This Charming Man" in November 1983. But for the pop kids, it was their first real sighting of George Michael and Andrew Ridgeley – in a blur of denim, espadrilles and waxed chests – that hit the spot... the moment when Wham! made their debut on *Top of the Pops* on 4 November 1982.

In an era where it was often deemed fashionable to send up a *Top of the Pops* slot by treating it with a whiff of poorly mimed disdain, Wham! upended expectations by putting on a performance of drilled, military precision. In fact the whole presentation of their second single "Young Guns (Go For It!)" was a deliberate handbrake to what was going on before and around them at the time. The New Romantics had been ruling the roost and had advocated an anti-punk philosophy of "more is more" – the frills, the foundation, the fancy synthesizers, everything had to be over the top and in your face.

But the new thing on the block in 1982 was what British journalist Robert Elms had dubbed "hard times chic": dress down, keep it simple, times are tough, play the system. With their simple denim, noticeable lack of socks and rapped kitchen-sink drama about the dangers of settling down versus the freedom of the single life, Wham! hit the mood with carefree yet chilling accuracy. Flanked by backing singers Shirlie Holliman (now Kemp) and Dee C. Lee – though they didn't actually appear on the record – for sheer exuberance, sheer energy, sheer *cheek*, Wham! were hard to beat.

But after a peerless run of singles with Wham! George Michael managed to take things even further. *Much* further. As a solo star, he cut a path through the following decades, cracking America with what seemed like almost nonchalant ease. Along with the sales came the respect of his peers and those who had inspired him in the first place: "Not only was he a good friend, but he was probably one of the most brilliant songwriters this country's ever produced, and certainly one of the best vocalists ever," Sir Elton John said in February 2017. "One of the best in the world."

But accompanying all that talent was a sense that George Michael – despite all his wealth and success – was still *one of us*; he screwed up sometimes, just like we do. The difference being that our screw-ups don't get splashed across the front pages of the national and international press. This focus on him as a person – a very *fallible* person – was something he handled with varying degrees of success. "To be part of people's lives, as an artist, that's obviously what I dreamed of," he once said. "But my God, I wish I could cope with the other stuff the way other people do. I wish I'd been born with that particular suit of armour. Because I wasn't."

Despite being hounded over his sexuality and drug-taking – and pilloried for his politics and his stance on the Iraq War – George Michael seemed able to get back on his feet no matter how many times he was knocked down. And we loved him for it.

As a new century came and went, he continued to create music and controversy in equal measure, but there was a sense that he was by now perfectly placed to be ushered into the section of British celebrity marked "National Treasure" with very little objection.

But at the end of 2016 – a year that obituary writers will remember as a defining period – we lost him. After 12 months of relentless and shocking celebrity deaths, George Michael's seemed to be felt by the public in a very different way. David Bowie was adored, admired and revered. George Michael, on the other hand, was *loved*.

His story feels personal to us in a way that most musicians' lives rarely do – so too do his songs, his image, his life and his times. In his early years he gave us the freedom to have a good time – later, the freedom to think about things differently. But he always gave us the freedom to *feel*.

So here, in pictures and in words is George Michael's story: *Freedom*.

OPPOSITE The singer posing in a studio photoshoot in 1982.

OVERLEAF The Japanese/Australasian leg of his Faith World Tour in 1988.

IMMIGRANT SONG

When the boy born Georgios Kyriacos Panayiotou arrived at Bushey Meads School in Hertfordshire in 1975, the teacher looked around the class, wondering who would be willing to look after the youngster. "New kid?" fellow pupil Andrew Ridgeley would later recall thinking when the youngster walked in. "Give him to me!"

Had it not been for Ridgeley's gregarious nature – very much apparent, even at that age – then it's possible that Panayiotou's talents as a singer, songwriter, producer and performer on a global scale under the name of George Michael would have been less likely to come to the fore. Maybe they wouldn't have come out at all. "It changed my life," he later said about being taken under the Ridgeley wing. "It changed so many things. Without Andrew I would have been in a totally different place right now."

Ridgeley was also responsible for Georgios's playground nickname – Yog.

George Michael's background was steeped in the ethics of hard work and self-improvement:

ABOVE A snap from the family album: George aged five in 1968.

OPPOSITE From a photo shoot in 1983. This image, as well as others from the shoot, appeared in *Smash Hits* magazine.

"I'm a very typical second-generation immigrant. If I got anything from my father's side, it was the presumption that you go and you move up. I was definitely supposed to be an accountant or a lawyer. There was never any suggestion that I was going to be anything other than an upwardly mobile child."

His Greek-Cypriot father, Kyriacos Panayiotou, had arrived in Britain in 1953, initially getting work as a waiter in north London. As his ambition grew and he became an assistant restaurant manager, his name shrunk – he simplified it to Jack Panos. When he married English girl Lesley Harrison they set up home in a small flat in Finchley; first they had two daughters, Yioda and Melanie, then, on 25 June 1963, a son: Georgios.

Dad had by now progressed from being a waiter to being the owner of his own restaurant, but money was still tight and mum Lesley had to look after the children, work in Jack's restaurant and do shifts in a local fish and chip shop: "Mum said it was the most disgusting period of her life," George would later recall. "She couldn't get the smell of fish off her hair and her skin. Poor cow would come home, look after us, then go and work in my dad's restaurant.

She was just exhausted. She had two jobs, had three children to look after and an extremely unreasonable husband who expected her to work at the restaurant every night, otherwise he'd never see her."

GEORGE AND ANDREW

George's presence at Bushey Meads School was as a result of an early instance of him standing up to his father, who, in the spirit of family upward mobility, had wanted George to go to a private school. George had refused – and that's how he found himself sitting next to Andrew Ridgeley.

Ridgeley, like George, was the product of an Anglo-immigrant marriage; his father was from Cairo. "I thought he was pretty loud," George recalled in 1983 when asked about his initial impression of Ridgeley. "Brash. I thought, *There's a boy I want to sit next to*. Actually, that's not true. I was *ordered* to."

The childhood pictures of George Michael tell a story in themselves: Michael's smile is hesitant, his sweaters look as uncomfortable as he does, his demeanour is very much set at "flying-under-the-radar". "I came from a very oppressive household where it was all keep your voice down, your father's tired," he said in 2004. "That's a great basis for someone who wants to build themselves as a singer. Because what fascinates people about singing is that your presence in the world is louder than everything else."

His new friend from Bushey Meads School couldn't have been more different: "Andrew's real ambition when we met was to be a footballer or a pop star," was how George remembered his friend's attitude to life. "He knew he didn't want to go to university, he wanted to start a band."

ABOVE AND OPPOSITE Childhood innocence: more photos from the family collection.

MUSICAL AMBITIONS

Like Ridgeley, Georgios also had musical ambitions: "I don't remember telling [my parents] I was going to be a pop star. They just knew I was obsessed by music and that was what I wanted to do."

George's dad couldn't understand it – in his view, his son "couldn't sing to save his life".

Unlike Ridgeley, George had taken the time to study an instrument, learning the violin as well as becoming a good enough drummer to audition for local bands. He would also regularly go busking for loose change with friend and neighbour David Mortimer. Ridgeley preferred to dance, and roped in his friend to see the recently released film *Saturday Night Fever*, which had an electrifying effect on young Georgios. "George had a lack of confidence with his physicality, his own personal aesthetic," Ridgeley would later say. "That was all solved by

Saturday Night Fever. Completely cured it. Dancing was a means of self-expression for George. We used to go to London, to really dive little discos, and there we would dance. We went to a lot of local places near Bushey, too. But we were not too keen on those because you could never tell when you were going to get a bottle in your face. We practised our dancing at home, we practised our dancing when we went out, we got all our moves together. We were very much into the pair-dancing thing."

Dancing was great – but what Ridgeley wanted was to be in a *band*. He cajoled and encouraged his friend to get involved. A loose collective formed, centred around Ridgeley, his brother Paul, school friend Andrew Leaver and David Mortimer. The question was: What kind of band would they be?

The late 1970s in Britain saw youth culture exploding into different directions and cults like never before. After punk, the streets were awash with teenage tribes of every style, attitude and musical persuasion. The release of the film *Quadrophenia* sparked a mod revival that mirrored the original movement in its clothes, scooters and violence.

ABOVE The duo's first live appearance during their Club Fantastic Tour in 1983.

OPPOSITE This was taken by Gered Mankowitz in 1983. Wham! had just released their album *Fantastic* and "Club Tropicana" was heading up the charts.

OVERLEAF The pop sensation Wham!

"WE FELT IT HAD THE ENERGY, IT HAD EXUBERANCE AND IT WAS SHORT. IT WAS A NAME THAT SUITED A POP BAND AND THAT'S WHAT WE WANTED TO BE"

ANDREW RIDGELEY

Elsewhere, music weekly *Sounds* coined the term "New Wave of British Heavy Metal" to describe the growing number of young rock bands springing up across the country, spearheaded by the release of the debut EP by Iron Maiden. Not to be outdone, music paper rival the *NME* were championing post-punk: for them, the future lay in bands like Joy Division, Comsat Angels and Echo & The Bunnymen. The dress code was long macs, dark clothes and dour expressions. In London and Birmingham, ex-punks and Bowie fans were experimenting with new, more flamboyant styles that would be dubbed New Romantic. By way of contrast, skinhead culture was morphing into ska, spearheaded by 2 Tone Records and the label's first release "Gangsters/The Selecter". Too young to have been punks and seemingly unaware of the burgeoning New Romantic scene, the band of Bushey friends adopted the sound of ska and named the band The Executive.

WHAM!

The band recorded demos and made their live debut at the local Methodist hall in November 1979. "We were so full of confidence," Georgios recalled. "Even though we were really bad." As ever with young bands, members began to drift away, leaving Georgios and Andrew as a duo. The 18-year-olds' love of dancing continued through – Ridgeley's then girlfriend Shirlie Holliman would join them as they continued to work out bedroom routines that could be performed in clubs. Shirlie: "When I first met the boys together, they were such great friends. The humour, the music; that was the foundation for Wham! Also, George needed Andrew – he was the outgoing one, the funny one, the charming one."

Meanwhile, Georgios took odd jobs to appease his parents, even working at his dad's restaurant: "I hated every moment of it," he later said. "But it was a good exercise in knowing what I *didn't* want to do."

Attempts at songwriting continued. One tune in particular seemed to have potential, with words and melody by Georgios and some chords added by Ridgeley. It was called "Careless Whisper" and people who heard it seemed to think it was pretty good.

The funkier beats coming out of the London clubs – and their beloved *Saturday Night Fever* – began to seep into other songs and on to a demo. "The tape featured 'Wham Rap!' and 'Careless Whisper'," Ridgeley later recalled. "We made the tape with a couple of friends and a drum machine. George was singing, I played guitar."

"Wham Rap! (Enjoy What You Do)" sounded so good they took part of the title as their name. Andrew Ridgeley: "We felt it had the energy, it had exuberance and it was short. It was a name that suited a pop band and that's what we wanted to be."

With what seemed at the time to be an outrageous piece of good fortune, the duo's demo came across the desk of an up-and-coming local record executive. Mark Dean, who had previously said thanks but no thanks to a demo by The Executive, had convinced CBS to back his scheme to set up his own label, called Innervision, thanks to the success he'd had with the likes of ABC and Soft Cell. Dean was a young man in a hurry; he took the young duo to a local café and offered Wham! £500 to sign with him there and then.

They signed – and like his father before him, Georgios shortened and simplified his name. He became George Michael.

OPPOSITE Clad in denim and leather: George and Andrew in 1986.

OVERLEAF Wham! and their various styles and personalities.

STICK TOGETHER

"It's almost impossible to remember what happened at the beginning of Wham!" George Michael would later say. "It was happening at such an outrageous speed. We worked constantly through those four years, so it's all a bit of a blur."

The blur began as Wham! prepared to release their debut single "Wham Rap! (Enjoy What You Do)" in June 1982, opening up their account with a funked-up tale of being a soul boy on the dole. Rap in Britain had yet to gain any kind of real foothold in terms of home-grown releases. Despite the UK chart success of The Sugarhill Gang's "Rapper's Delight" in 1979 and Blondie's crossover hit "Rapture" in 1981, Britain seemed shy of attempting what appeared to be a curiously American art form. The Clash had been the Brit pioneers, incorporating rap into their music as early as 1980 with "The Magnificent Seven" on their *Sandinista!* album. Adam Ant even had a go with his less than convincing "Ant Rap" in 1981.

British rap was virtually non-existent when into these choppy waters strode Wham!

"We actually had a very strong sense of doing something different, which really didn't get appreciated at the time," the newly named George Michael would state. "There's a really strong tongue-in-cheek element to the first three singles and we were hailed as being some kind of social commentators for our generation… i.e. being on the dole. Actually, I hadn't – Andrew had been on the dole for years borrowing money off me."

Although the song wasn't a hit first-time around, it garnered them some evening airplay on Radio 1 and got them a piece in style mag *The Face*, which clearly loved their stripped-down leather jacket and jeans "hard times chic" image. The pair were sent out on a tour of the clubs to do mimed public appearances along with Shirlie Holliman and former EMI session singer Dee C. Lee. "Those club tours were extremely hard work," Lee would later remember. "Sometimes five or six shows a night. But we enjoyed all of it. As it was a new and fresh experience it didn't really feel like work. We were always surprised by the fantastic reaction from the audiences and became more confident with every show."

ABOVE The iconic image from 1983 of George and Andrew locked in an arm-wrestle.

OPPOSITE A shot from the photo shoot with Gered Mankowitz in 1983. The image appeared in *Smash Hits* magazine.

The single failed to breach the Top 100, but undeterred they stuck with the rap format – and a penchant for brackets and exclamation marks – for their second release "Young Guns (Go For It!)" four months later. The release warranted a fresh photo shoot and George unveiled a new look – three-quarter-length jeans. He can be seen staring moodily at the camera, a single plucked eyebrow raised as he poses sitting on a reversed wooden chair.

The live club PAs continued and it was at one such event that they were noticed by a BBC TV talent booker. "Someone from the BBC spotted us in [London nightclub] Stringfellows and invited us on to [kids' BBC TV show] *Saturday Superstore*," Holliman would later recall. "It all escalated from there, really."

TOP OF THE CHARTS

The exposure on *Saturday Superstore*, fronted by Radio 1 DJ Mike Read, got them noticed at the BBC; so much so that when another act dropped out of *Top of the Pops* Wham! were invited to fill in. "Young Guns (Go For It!)" had been

lurking just outside of the UK Top 40 – after THAT high-energy performance it climbed to Number 3, spending 17 weeks in the charts. "I remember going shopping in Watford with George after the programme had finished, and we were recognized," said Holliman. "People were staring and pointing at us."

Both ends of the music-press spectrum gave the single the thumbs up – from the *New Musical Express* to *Smash Hits*. Even the doyen of alternative music John Peel loved them and played "Young Guns" on his late-night show. "George Michael has a strong pop-soul voice and he writes vexingly catchy songs," was Peel's view.

Innervision re-released "Wham Rap! (Enjoy What You Do)" in February 1983 to capitalize on the success and this time around the single reached Number 8, staying in the UK singles chart a total of eight weeks. The band put in another highly focused performance on *Top of the Pops* but this time it was a slightly less democratic affair – George was front and centre, while Andrew, Shirlie and Dee C. stayed in the dry ice-shrouded background.

ABOVE Posing at a photo shoot following the release of "Young Guns (Go For It)".

OPPOSITE Wham! on stage in London in 1984.

OVERLEAF Helen "Pepsi" DeMacque, Shirlie Holliman, George and Andrew on stage in 1985.

"I WANT US TO BE THE BIGGEST GROUP IN THE WORLD"

ANDREW RIDGELEY

"BUT IT'S AMAZING HOW MUCH MORE COMPLICATED IT BECAME BECAUSE I DIDN'T COME OUT IN THE EARLY DAYS. I OFTEN WONDER IF MY CAREER WOULD HAVE TAKEN A DIFFERENT PATH IF I HAD"

GEORGE MICHAEL

Andrew Ridgeley's role in proceedings would come under constant scrutiny throughout his time in Wham! and beyond. It seemed a mystery to many as to why he was there. To George it was simple – Ridgeley was the image of the group, representing all the things that he himself wasn't: "Between the two of us we got it sorted out very, very early," George would later say of their professional relationship. "In terms of the songwriting, Andrew said, 'Off you go.' He said, 'I want us to be the biggest group in the world and I think that the way to do it is to let you go with it.'"

So George had to get on with the business of writing hit songs – the pressure was on for three in a row. Their next release would be the logical next step in their "autobiographical" trio of singles: this time around they weren't just soul boys on the dole, seeking out the single life... they were "Bad Boys". Despite being loved by fans and proving to be their biggest hit to date – getting to Number 2 in May 1983 – George always frowned upon the song: "I wrote to a formula for 'Bad Boys', trying to replicate something else," he later admitted. "That's something I've never done before and have never done since."

THE FIRST ALBUM

Less than two months later, Wham! released their first album – *Fantastic*. It was a brief eight-track affair that included one of their oldest songs "Come On" and a cover of "Love Machine" by The Miracles that very much fitted in with their love 'em and leave 'em image. "Careless Whisper" was left to one side, for fear that its tale of remorse for a love lost was out of step with their "Love Machine" image. Further attempts would be made to record the track – its time was yet to come. For many, the real point of interest on the album would prove to be new song "Club Tropicana", which opened up side two. The pumped-up, self-referencing "social commentary" of their first singles was abandoned for a gently satirical take on the fashion for Club 18–30 "sun, sea and sex" holidays.

The tempting tale of a holiday hideaway with drinks, girls and fun in endless supply was set to a gentler, finger-clicking beat. The song's bikini-and-Speedo-heavy video was filmed in Ibiza; while they were there George confided in his bandmates that he thought he might be gay – and he wanted to tell the world about it.

"GEORGE MICHAEL HAS A STRONG POP-SOUL VOICE AND HE WRITES VEXINGLY CATCHY SONGS"

JOHN PEEL

He was counselled to keep the news to himself, with Ridgeley particularly firm in his advice that George shouldn't tell his father. "I had very little fear about it, but basically my straight friends talked me out of it. I think they thought as I was bisexual, there was no need to. But it's amazing how much more complicated it became because I didn't come out in the early days. I often wonder if my career would have taken a different path if I had."

The feel-good vibe of both the song and the video pushed it to Number 4 in the singles chart and helped propel *Fantastic* to Number 1 in the albums chart. The £500 sweetener to get Wham! to sign with Innervision must have felt like money well spent. An iconic image at the time was of George and Andrew arm-wrestling, locked in grim combat together. The reality was that these bad boys were united in their unhappiness about the way their affairs were being run by Innervision – the wages they were on barely matched the odd job and dole money they'd been on before they were signed. While the row continued, Innervision put out a holding track – "Club Fantastic Megamix" – but the writing was on the wall. "There's a lot of legal difficulties at the moment, which is why we haven't got a single out," George said at the time. "Which is a shame. We're trying to sort these things out."

Meanwhile, Dee C. Lee left to work on her own solo material and with Paul Weller's Style Council, to be replaced by Pepsi DeMacque. The ship needed steadying if the success was to continue.

THE FIRST TOUR

The first Wham! tour opened up in the autumn of 1983 with a two-night run of shows in Aberdeen. Subverting the usual rock gig clichés, the show featured a DJ rather than a support act and a short film was shown halfway through the main act's set to give the boys a breather. Photos of the opening night on 9 October show a sea of outstretched female arms as George dances at the front of stage, dressed entirely in white and wearing alarmingly short shorts. Inside these shorts was a strategically placed shuttlecock, which was promptly whipped out so the boys could play badminton on stage. Tour DJ Gary Crowley: "It was George who decided to take out one of his shuttlecocks and I remember him sort of circling it around his belly button and running it up and down his leg and picking up

the sweat." The shuttlecock would then be launched into the crowd. Not too subtle, but undoubtedly effective.

But behind the scenes another game was being played out – that of extracting Wham! from their contract with Innervision. Simon Napier-Bell was approached – he was one of the music industry's wiliest operators who'd done wonders for the likes of Marc Bolan and Japan. Napier-Bell felt that if he was given free reign, he could turn Wham! into one of the biggest acts in the world.

ABOVE George and Andrew relishing in their new-found glory.

OPPOSITE Time for a game of badminton – George whips out a shuttlecock from inside his white shorts.

OVERLEAF All four members of the group onstage, stirring up the crowd.

TOP OF A DREAM

After a deal was struck to shift Wham! to the Epic label, they re-emerged in May 1984 with a new injection of cash and a song with more mainstream appeal: "Wake Me Up Before You Go-Go".

Out went the bad boy pose, the raps and the social commentary; in came fun, frivolity and fifties beats. George Michael: "I just wanted to make a really energetic pop record that had all the best elements of 1950s and 60s records, combined with our attitude and our approach, which is obviously more up-tempo and a lot younger than some of those records. It's one of those tracks that gets rid of a lot of your own personal influences; it reminds me of so many different records that I couldn't actually nail them down."

If Wham! had seemed focused before, it now felt like they had a laser sight pinpointing the top of the charts. Along with the irresistible bounce of the song, they had a video that featured day-glo clothing, jitterbug dancing and some of the shortest shorts ever seen on TV. The band had one more secret weapon – the iconic CHOOSE LIFE T-shirts they wore, created by the highly political British designer Katharine Hamnett.

The song gave Wham! their first-ever UK Number 1 and it stayed there for two weeks, reason enough for celebration. When "Wake Me Up Before You Go-Go" did the same in the US, it took them to another level: "There's no doubt that our ambition is to become the biggest band in the world and I think it's within our reach," George said as Wham! prepared to tour America for the first time. "Why not? There's nothing to be ashamed of."

In 1984, there was a battle being fought on Britain's high streets – Wham!'s CHOOSE LIFE tops versus Frankie Goes To Hollywood's "Relax" version. The Liverpool band's second single "Two Tribes" had spent nine weeks at the top of the charts – who could possibly knock them off? The battle of Frankie versus Wham! was settled when a revamped "Careless Whisper" – credited as a George solo single – took the top slot in the first week of August.

What's more, the song went to Number 1 in a total of 25 countries – including the US – selling more than six million copies.

ABOVE Wham! in 1984, the same year as the release of the hit song "Careless Whisper".

OPPOSITE The boys performing on the ITV show *Razzamatazz*.

With its roaring sax solo opening, artful guilty lyric and whisper-to-a-yell vocal, it became the archetypal swoonsome 1980s ballad. *Everyone* loved it... apart, it seemed, from George Michael. "I'm still a bit puzzled why it's made such an impression on people," George would say in 2009. "Is it because so many people have cheated on their partners? Is that why they connect with it? I have no idea, but it's ironic that this song – which has come to define me in some way – should have been written right at the beginning of my career when I was still so young. I was only 17 and didn't really know much about anything – and certainly nothing much about relationships."

MAKING IT BIG

Despite being a George solo track, "Careless Whisper" was included as part of Wham!'s second album, the prophetically titled *Make It Big*. The album was largely recorded in France. Ridgeley was, as ever, charmingly honest about the reasons why: "We chose the south of France for a couple of reasons

– one because our accountant advised us to go there for tax purposes. The other was that it's within easy reach of London, so that [if] anything that crops up like TV or radio, we can make it there in an hour or so."

Despite Ridgeley getting a co-writing credit on "Careless Whisper", there was no doubt by now as to who was in the driving seat – *Make It Big* was not only largely written by George, he produced it, too: "I was doing something remarkable as a 21-year-old kid; I was a producer and an arranger and I knew how to make these records and how to make them jump out of the radio."

The album went to Number 1 in the UK and the US and also spawned the massive hit "Freedom". George was everywhere – as shown by a brief snatched interview he gave during a recording session held on 25 November at Sarm West Studios in London.

ABOVE George and Andrew performing in 1984.

OPPOSITE The singer's first foray into producing, with the release of *Make It Big* in 1984.

"I'm absolutely exhausted, it was supposed to be my day off but... but good cause. The management told me that Bob was getting it together and it seemed like a really great idea. I didn't actually know it was going to be so many people – but, the more the better."

"DO THEY KNOW IT'S CHRISTMAS?"

Bob was of course Bob Geldof, and the recording was for the charity single "Do They Know It's Christmas?" George joined the likes of Bono, Sting and Phil Collins to appear on the song, which it was hoped would raise around £70,000 for famine relief in Ethiopia. That aim was outstripped many times over, helped in no little part by George's decision to donate the royalties from Wham!'s double-A side "Last Christmas/Everything She Wants" to the appeal. It would be an early example of George's extraordinary generosity, something that would continue throughout his life – while many saw him as a frivolous, decadent pop star, he was secretly giving away millions.

THE BIG TOUR

Meanwhile, a pre-Christmas UK tour – The Big Tour – shored up Wham!'s reputation as one of the biggest acts around. They ended the year with a four-night stand at Wembley Arena. George couldn't resist a dig at his pop rivals: "I think we're the most entertaining pop act on the road at the moment," he said. "I saw Duran Duran, Culture Club, and Spandau Ballet last year, and I think the people who see our gigs go away having had a better time."

Despite their success in the US, manager Simon Napier-Bell felt they could do more. Never a man to use mere promotional device when an outrageous stunt could be pulled, Napier-Bell and Wham!'s co-manager Jazz Summers came up with a ruse to garner Wham! what they hoped would be acres of publicity: as part of a world tour, they would play an unprecedented set of shows in China.

ABOVE The stars of "Do They Know It's Christmas?". The song raised millions for the famine in Ethiopia.

OPPOSITE AND OVERLEAF The first Western band to play in China: Wham!

"THE SINGERS WERE ALL MOVING A LOT AND IT WAS VERY LOUD. WE WERE USED TO PEOPLE WHO STOOD STILL WHEN THEY PERFORMED. ALL THE YOUNG PEOPLE WERE AMAZED..."

KAN LIJUN

The idea behind the shows in Beijing and the southern city of Guangzhou in April 1985 was that the Chinese authorities would get to show how their country had changed after the Cultural Revolution – in exchange, Wham! would receive international press coverage, particularly in America. The plan came with a price tag, though – Wham! would be footing the bill. Napier-Bell would later claim that the whole enterprise cost them in the region of £1 million.

Kan Lijun served as the on-stage host at Wham!'s concert in Beijing, introducing them to the crowd who had paid the 1985 equivalent of about 50 pence for a ticket. "No one had ever seen anything like that before," she said. "The singers were all moving a lot and it was very loud. We were used to people who stood still when they performed. All the young people were amazed and everybody was tapping their feet. Of course the police weren't happy and they were scared there would be riots. One time, people were excited after a sports event and they flipped a car."

There were no riots but, publicity aside, the trip wasn't exactly the cunning wheeze it set out to be: a documentary film about the trip shot by left-field British director Lindsay Anderson was judged to be "a shambles" by Napier-Bell, and hopes that it would prove to be a money-spinner were to be very wide of the mark. There was no benefit to be had in terms of record sales in China and Wham! had already achieved huge success in the USA without the aid of a highly expensive vanity project. If anyone had proved to be wily it was the Chinese government, who managed to benefit most from the ensuing publicity... and got Wham! to pay for it. Now *that's* clever.

ABOVE LEFT George in demand by reporters.

ABOVE RIGHT George and Andrew holding koala motif sweaters while on tour. Behind them are awards for record sales, including one for their first album, *Fantastic*.

OPPOSITE On stage during The Big Tour, which took in Japan, Australia, China and the US.

LIVE AID

George was to be involved in an even bigger project that really would connect on a worldwide level on his return – Live Aid. If it was worldwide publicity he wanted, then he could have saved himself a lot of time and money and waited for the event billed as the "Global Jukebox" on 13 July 1985 in London. Nearly two billion people watched Queen, U2, David Bowie and many more perform at Wembley Stadium, as Bob Geldof's plan to raise £70,000 for Ethiopia reached epic proportions. George duetted with his hero Elton John that day, singing "Don't Let The Sun Go Down On Me". It was a mature performance from George – Andrew Ridgeley stayed very much in the background. A huge event for a serious cause, for many it seemed to beg the question as to how long the fun-loving, frolicksome idea of Wham! could continue. Ridgeley himself seemed more aware of this than anyone: "We didn't really see how he [George] could take the concept of Wham! and turn it into adulthood. We were right."

LEFT George Michael, Harvey Goldsmith, Bono, Paul McCartney and Freddie Mercury performing "Feed The World" during the finale of the Live Aid Concert at Wembley in 1985.

OVERLEAF Farewell from Wham! The frenzied crowds and the duo on stage at The Final – their goodbye concert – Wembley Stadium, 28 June 1986.

THE FINAL

After a tour of the US – and racking up another UK Number 1 with the solo outing "A Different Corner" – George decided that the time had indeed come to end Wham! "The Edge Of Heaven" would be their final UK single and a concert at Wembley on 28 June 1986 – dubbed The Final – would be their last-ever live show. It turned out to be a strange, sprawling affair with some bizarre choices of support acts: the first person to play was Gary Glitter; Elton John appeared dressed as Ronald McDonald and Duran Duran's Simon Le Bon appeared as a backing singer. The China film – heavily re-cut – also got its first airing.

It proved to be an emotional affair for George: "I was drinking a lot and generally feeling run-down" was how he described his mood going into the gig. "I don't think I rose above it, even on the day of The Final. With a genuine depression it doesn't matter how good the highs are, there's an undercurrent of depression that doesn't go away. I really enjoyed the day and the concert, but looking at the pictures of it, I can see that something was wrong, even with Andrew. He looks more drawn than he did on pictures [taken] only a year before. He was doing a lot of drink and stuff and there were worries on his mind, I suppose."

"I didn't enjoy it as much as other shows," was Ridgeley's view. "The whole period leading up to it was a difficult one for me. I kept thinking, when the encore's done… *that's it*. And that was a really difficult concept to get to grips with."

The pair had gone from a couple of teenage hopefuls signing a deal in a greasy-spoon café to just about the biggest band in the world in the space of barely four years. There would never be another band quite like Wham! and no one seemed to realize that quite as strongly as George Michael. "My time with Wham! were the happiest years of my life," he said later. "When I listen to our records I hear two young men who are having the best time they would ever have. It's amazing, the joy in it, the spirit of it. I listen to myself singing in Wham! and I think, 'Who is that person?' And I know who he is and I know who those two boys are – two kids at the top of a dream."

ABOVE The boys from Wham! during their last show – an emotional event for both singers.

OPPOSITE George performing with Elton John, dressed as Ronald McDonald, at The Final concert.

OVERLEAF George singing at The Final.

"WHEN I LISTEN TO OUR RECORDS I HEAR TWO YOUNG MEN WHO ARE HAVING THE BEST TIME THEY WOULD EVER HAVE. IT'S AMAZING, THE JOY IN IT, THE SPIRIT OF IT"

GEORGE MICHAEL

DOING A GEORGE MICHAEL

It was a time of change – the first thing that went was the management team of Simon Napier-Bell and Jazz Summers. George cut his ties after finding out about a deal to sell the company that managed him to a firm with strong South African interests – for the politically aware George such a move was unacceptable. Napier-Bell would later paint the deal as a terrific money-making scam, designed to make cash from the group even though they were calling it a day: "If you've spent three years making the biggest group in the world and you know they're going to break up," the flamboyant manager later said, "then you sell them to a bunch of lousy South Africans, don't you?"

George spent time in the US, sorting out his affairs and taking on a new manager, Rob Kahane, who'd already been acting as his booking agent. Andrew Ridgeley

ABOVE AND OVERLEAF Aretha and George singing their iconic Grammy-winning hit "I Knew You Were Waiting (For Me)".

OPPOSITE George at a photo shoot, circa 1989.

came out to visit him. Ridgeley had been quoted in the British press saying the spilt had taken him by complete surprise – he was still being managed by Simon Napier-Bell at this stage. The visit proved the pair were still friends: "Our relationship was going to have to reach some kind of other level and that was tough," George later admitted. "I had no idea how much I was going to miss [his] support or how close to lunacy I would feel without that support."

The next series of moves that George would make would become the textbook of how to move from a teen idol to a serious artist – so much so that "doing a George Michael" became music industry jargon for the best way of transitioning heartthrobs into international household names.

The first move was to pair him with a singer who could give him grown-up cachet and provide that all-important "he can really sing" stamp of credibility. Aretha Franklin, the undisputed Queen of Soul, was the ideal candidate.

"I NOTED HE HAD A VERY UNIQUE SOUND, VERY DIFFERENT FROM ANYTHING THAT WAS OUT THERE. DID I KNOW IT WOULD BE A HIT? YOU NEVER KNOW THAT UNTIL THE PEOPLE HAVE SPOKEN"

ARETHA FRANKLIN

Their duet single "I Knew You Were Waiting (For Me)" showed that George could hold his own against the considerable firepower of Aretha. It was a Number 1 on both sides of the Atlantic. Franklin benefited, too; the song was her first US Number 1 for 20 years, her only ever British chart-topper, and extended her run of UK hits well into the 1990s. "The first time I heard George was when he was with Wham! and I liked him then," She later said. "I noted he had a very unique sound, very different from anything that was out there. Did I know it would be a hit? You never know that until the people have spoken. We waited for the people to speak and it went to the Top 10 and won a Grammy."

The link-up with Franklin worked perfectly and changed the way George was seen by both the public and the critics. Meanwhile, George's look was changing too: his hair had become a little less "80s", he sported designer stubble and he'd reverted to his old "biker" look with a studded leather jacket.

The next section in the How To Become A Mature Artist playbook was: "Create a Controversy". This is exactly what George did with his single "I Want Your Sex", released in June 1987, with the BBC playing right into his hands and banning the single from daytime airplay. *Perfect.* In the accompanying video, George played it straight and sexy, with acres of flesh and lingerie on display from American model Kathy Jeung, who was regularly described in the press at the time as his girlfriend.

But as ever, innuendo and rumour surrounded George: "His real worry was that some personal things were going to come out," said Simon Napier-Bell just after he stopped acting as the singer's manager. "If he's gay and hiding it, he's brilliant. My feeling is that when he was a kid he was podgy and curly haired and wore glasses and he created from himself a good-looking guy. I think he's permanently terrified that one day he's going to wake up and look in the mirror and see the podgy face again."

George, meanwhile, was focused on his career – "I Want Your Sex" had done exactly what he'd wanted it to: "It launched my career in America with such a bang – no pun intended! I couldn't have wished for anything better to happen in that my career needed to go somewhere, needed to do an about turn."

OPPOSITE George performing at a concert in Australia in 1989.

OVERLEAF In February 1988, George Micheal embarked on his first solo tour – the Faith World Tour.

"I COULDN'T HAVE WISHED FOR ANYTHING BETTER TO HAPPEN IN THAT MY CAREER NEEDED TO GO SOMEWHERE, NEEDED TO DO AN ABOUT TURN"

GEORGE MICHAEL

FAITH

A whole heap of publicity, some healthy controversy and a Top 3 hit in Britain and the US was the perfect way to prepare the ground for George Michael as a "grown-up" artist and would pave the way for his solo album *Faith*, released in October 1987. Another way to signal a new level of maturity as a performer is range – and when the album's title track was released as a single, it showed just that. The Prince-style bump 'n' grind of "I Want Your Sex" was replaced with the stripped-down acoustic guitar and Bo Diddley beat of the title track.

The song introduced another iconic George look: mirror shades, ripped and bleached jeans, "revenge" leather jacket and an acre of stubble. Simple but very effective. But if George thought it would shed him of his teenybop image, he was sadly mistaken: "I deluded myself that I wasn't going to attract a whole new generation of girls with the whole *Faith* image. If you look at it I mean, what do you expect? You're waving your arse at the camera! It's quite a nice arse though…"

The album – produced by George, who also wrote every track apart from "Look At Your Hands", a co-write with old mate David Mortimer, now going by the name of David Austin –

was a smash. Despite only staying at Number 1 in Britain for a week, it took up residence at the top of the US charts for nearly three months and generated four Number 1 singles. George had wanted US success – he got it. But even he was shocked at the critical and commercial scale of it: "I honestly think that in America people overrated *Faith*. People were writing things and I was thinking… hold on a minute, I know it's not *that* good." Despite his misgivings, George had re-written the rule book, successfully making the transition from teen idol to grown-up artist: "People have this idea it's terribly easy to cross over. A lot of people took it at surface [level] and didn't acknowledge that all the way through the whole screaming kids market that we had, there was an undercurrent of older buyers, which made it much easier for me to cross over. The market is so much more ruthless now. People are so fickle; the turnover is so fast. It's fast food, the singles' market."

ABOVE George at a press conference in 1988, during his Faith World Tour.

OPPOSITE On stage during the Australasian/Japanese leg of the tour.

OVERLEAF The singer receiving attention from a makeup artist prior to appearing at a press conference during the tour.

ABOVE George performing in Earl's Court, London, 10 June 1988.

OPPOSITE Achieving the fame and success that he had hoped for – George on his Faith World Tour.

OPPOSITE AND OVERLEAF Nelson Mandela's 70th Birthday Tribute concert at Wembley Stadium, London, 11 June 1988. As well as George Michael, the big names at the concert included Dire Straits, Simple Minds, Whitney Houston and the Eurythmics.

"I HONESTLY THINK THAT IN AMERICA PEOPLE OVERRATED *FAITH*. PEOPLE WERE WRITING THINGS AND I WAS THINKING … HOLD ON A MINUTE, I KNOW IT'S NOT *THAT* GOOD"

GEORGE MICHAEL

UNDER SCRUTINY

The accompanying Faith World Tour started in Japan and snaked its way through Australia, Europe and North America. George briefly stepped off the treadmill in June 1988 to sing at the Nelson Mandela 70th Birthday Tribute at his home from home, Wembley Stadium.

George had achieved all the fame and success he'd ever hoped for. The trouble was, now he had what he wanted... he found that he really didn't like it. *At all*. "It's a very intense thing to go through for ten months, which is effectively what I did with *Faith*. By the end of it I was going insane. I had to negotiate a new relationship with celebrity that wasn't going to destroy me. I don't think there's any way I could control my ego enough to stop me from exploring the possibility of being the biggest-selling artist in the world."

Everywhere he went George was under intense scrutiny, particularly from the British newspapers. In Wham! George

– and more especially, Andrew – had been the source of endless good-time copy. The fun-loving Wham! boys had filled the pages of the tabloids with their antics, and journalists couldn't get enough of them. But now George had achieved massive success in the US, the British press seemed to turn on him – during one Faith Tour press conference in Rotterdam, he was asked by a journalist from the *Daily Mirror* if he'd had an AIDS test. George replied that he hadn't. The headline the following day was I LIVE IN FEAR OF AIDS by George Michael.

There wasn't even an attempt to be coy any more – the British tabloids wanted George to say he was gay: "I don't bother denying it anymore because I'm sick of denying it," he said in 1988. "What else are they going to do?"

As the end of the 1980s approached, it was a question that George was about to get an answer to.

CHAPTER FIVE

A VERY AMERICAN KIND OF BLASPHEMY

"I was intelligent enough to know that this was the wrong road," George would later reflect when he cast his mind back to the staggering success of *Faith*. "If I was looking for happiness I should not be trying to catch up with Michael Jackson or Madonna. Which is absolutely what I was intent on doing as a British star."

Another Grammy for Album of the Year... an Ivor Novello for Song of the Year... an MTV Video Vanguard award... George Michael had everything. But it wasn't making him happy. At the height of his despair over the gilded cage he found himself trapped in, even Frank Sinatra weighed in with some sage words of advice: "Come on, George, loosen up. Swing, man."

The fact that George seemed to resent his success didn't play well in the US, something he – with the

help of Ol' Blue Eyes himself – began to realize very quickly: "That's a very American kind of blasphemy, to question the level of your success," he would later observe.

Self-doubt and concern over huge success was not going to be an issue for George's former bandmate: in May 1990 Andrew Ridgeley released his first and only solo album. *Son of Albert* was panned by the critics and didn't trouble the Top 100; its accompanying single "Shake" – a perfectly reasonable slice of Album-oriented rock – got to Number 58 in the UK charts. "I'm convinced there were four hit records on that album", was George's view, supportive as ever. "It's such a shame."

Instead of calling his album *Son of Albert*, Ridgeley could have done worse than borrow the title of George's next release on 3 September 1990: *Listen Without Prejudice Vol. 1*. When George's record company heard what he'd recorded, they didn't like it.

OPPOSITE The MTV Video Vanguard award, won in 1989, was just one of the many awards George received during his career.

They liked what he decided to do next even less: "I won't be doing any videos or interviews for the foreseeable future," George declared. "I'm moving out of the promotional, selling myself side of things," he added. "It's pure sell. I'm stopping because I realized it was making me unhappy. The person I think I was when I started is not the same person as I am now... I don't really want to be visible any more."

George certainly wasn't visible in the video that accompanied the album's first single "Praying For Time". The promo clip for the Beatlesesque strummer only featured the song's sombre lyrics. This next single, "Waiting For That Day", was even more low-key. George was largely absent from the album's third single too – but this time there was something by way of compensation: supermodels. *Lots* of them.

FREEDOM

"Freedom! '90" featured Naomi Campbell, Linda Evangelista, Tatjana Patitz, Christy Turlington and Cindy Crawford – plus five male models – and became one of the defining promos of its time, despite the lack of its star singer. "If you're not going to appear in your own video," said George, "I'd say that's a fairly good consolation prize, those five gorgeous babes."

"George Michael decided he didn't want to play the game in the same way," Cindy Crawford would observe in 2017. "He wanted to make it his own game. I think it was a great message for people. I think people loved him more because of that."

The album – described by Q magazine as a "masterpiece" – still did brisk business despite George's reluctance to promote it in the traditional way, but it sold less than a third of the copies that *Faith* had shifted in the US. The next single, "Heal The Pain", stalled outside the UK Top 30 and didn't chart in the US at all. George didn't seem to care and went out on tour – not to promote his new album, but to sing a set of cover versions instead. There was a good reason for this seemingly cavalier attitude: he was in love.

RIGHT Elton and George performing together in the early 1990s.

RIO

At the Rock in Rio event in January 1991 – also notable for the fact that Andrew Ridgeley joined George on stage for the encore – something happened to the singer: "On the night of the first Rock in Rio concert in the Maracanã Stadium – 160,000 people, the largest audience I'd ever played in front of – in the front there was this guy at the right-hand side of the stage that just fixed me with this look. He was so cute. I was so distracted by him that I stayed away from that side of the stage. That was the moment my life changed."

George fell for fashion designer Anselmo Feleppa and immediately introduced him to his friends – it would be George's first true love affair: "It was just like, wow, I've met someone that I actually think I'm going to fall in love with, rather than just want their body for a while. Anselmo was the first time I loved someone unselfishly, where it really was about them."

Things seemed to going George's way again; a live duet with Elton John on "Don't Let The Sun Go Down On Me" proved to be a huge success, which meant that the pressure to make him toe the line by his record company eased a little: "For a while everything was OK with Sony," he later said. "The single with Elton was a massive hit worldwide. I guess you'd call it the calm before the storm."

But tragically, six months into their relationship, Anselmo told George he was ill and was going to have an HIV test. "I remember the moment when he told me about the test he'd been advised to have," George later recalled. "I remember him leaving the house. I remember looking at the sky and saying... Don't you dare do this to me."

George would later remember going home for Christmas while Anselmo took the test in Brazil. The singer was left waiting to hear the potentially devastating news, powerless to do anything: "I was sat at the Christmas table not knowing whether this man that I was in love with – this man that the people sat around the table *didn't even know about* – was terminally ill. And not knowing, therefore, if I was potentially terminally ill. It was possibly the loneliest time in my life."

FREDDIE

George would channel this frustration into his 1992 performance at the Freddie Mercury Tribute Concert in April. Mercury had died in November, little more than 24 hours after releasing a statement saying that he had AIDS. Five months later the likes of Guns N' Roses, David Bowie and the remaining members of Queen gathered at Wembley Stadium to honour his memory and raise money for a newly formed AIDS charity, the Mercury Phoenix Foundation. Anselmo Feleppa was in the crowd that night as George performed. "I went out there knowing two things – I had to honour Freddie Mercury and I had to pray for Anselmo... I wanted to die inside. It was overwhelming for me. I think what it did was create one of the best performances of my career."

"TOO FUNKY"

George's pent-up anger would be channelled in other ways too – towards his record company. A proposed *Listen Without Prejudice Vol. 2* was shelved, with George donating the album sessions' glaringly commercial track "Too Funky" to another AIDS awareness project, the 1992 *Red Hot + Dance* compilation album. Released as a single, "Too Funky" was a sizeable hit and featured another supermodel-heavy video, with George making the briefest of cameos as a director. But the album – to which he donated three tracks in all – was not so successful. Again, George felt his record company wasn't supporting him as an artist.

ABOVE During the "Too Funky" video shoot, in Paris, 1992.

OPPOSITE Tyra Banks, Linda Evangelista, George Michael, Eva Herzigova and Beverly Peele pose during the "Too Funky" shoot.

"IF I WAS LOOKING
FOR HAPPINESS
I SHOULD NOT
BE TRYING
TO CATCH UP
WITH MICHAEL
JACKSON OR
MADONNA. WHICH
IS ABSOLUTELY
WHAT I WAS
INTENT ON
DOING AS A
BRITISH STAR"

GEORGE MICHAEL

LEFT Lionel Richie, Whoopi Goldberg and George Michael perform on stage during at The Concert Benefiting The Elizabeth Taylor AIDS Foundation at Madison Square Garden, New York City on 11 October 1992.

SONY TROUBLES

By this stage, Sony was his "employer" and George decided he wanted to quit. Sony pointed out that contractually he had another decade of work for them ahead. He tried and failed to reach an agreement with them for him to be released from his contract.

In March 1993, Anselmo Feleppa died. Two things happened – first George came out to his family. "He never displayed any disappointment or homophobia," George said when asked about his father's reaction. "I'm sure he felt it, and it was hard for him, but he didn't lay any of it on to me, which I have to thank him for. This is sad, but I do feel success can negate a parent's disappointment. I genuinely feel that although his son is gay and not going to give him any grandkids, my dad's consolation is that I have done well in life."

The other thing that happened was that George decided to take his fight with his record company to the courts. "The Sony court case was a perfectly good place to put my anger," he later admitted. "Would I have been angry enough to take them on [if Anselmo hadn't died]? I've got a feeling that the answer to that is probably no."

The case opened in October of that year – George's fury hadn't lessened in the months since Anselmo's death and he would run and play squash before and after the court proceedings to try to flush the negative energy out of his system. It's believed that Sony had wanted to settle at the eleventh hour but, sensing he had the upper hand, George chose to have his day in court. The case would in fact drag on well into 1994 before a decision was finally reached: the judge ruled in Sony's favour – George had lost.

Standing on the court steps, he made a statement to the press through clenched teeth: "I have no right to resign," he said. "In fact, there is no such thing as resignation for an artist in the music industry. Effectively, you sign a piece of paper at the beginning of your career and you are expected to live with that decision, good or bad, for the rest of your professional life."

With the case over – an appeal was launched, but it seemed almost half-hearted – George had nowhere to direct his feelings over the death of Anselmo. Instead of directing his hurt and anger at the record industry he decided to channel it into in a song.

ABOVE George Michael speaking to the press during his failed court battle to be released from his Sony record contract in 1994.

OPPOSITE Outside court after losing his battle. George is wearing an AIDS ribbon.

CHAPTER SIX

WHAT WERE YOU THINKING?

"Jesus To A Child" broke a two-year-long dry spell for George. The song was unashamedly about Anselmo Feleppa. "I was so excited that I'd been able to put my feelings for him into words," he said. "The catharsis for me was massive."

George was so excited by the song he performed it at the MTV Europe Music Awards just days after he'd written it. It would mark the start of a creative path that would eventually lead to the album *Older*. Change was, once again, in the air – he dispensed with the services of his manager Rob Kahane and finally negotiated his release from Sony. His look had changed too – George now sported a "French crop" hairstyle that sent men scurrying to hairdressers with a picture of the singer for their barber to copy.

The new songs came slowly – by George's own admission their creation took place in a cloud of marijuana smoke – and "Jesus To A Child" wasn't released as a single until January 1996. It was a huge hit in both Britain and the US. The accompanying video was filled with downbeat images of young

men clinging to each other, surrounded by flames. In George's mind he wasn't hiding his sexuality from anyone – the press disagreed: "Until you sit down in front of the press and say, 'I am gay', you're not considered to be out," was George's view. "And I wasn't going to do that."

The album *Older* was released to strong reviews on the DreamWorks label – the label's first release before putting out an eclectic roster of material from artists like Rufus Wainwright and Randy Newman and by comedian Chris Rock. "The kind of optimism I showed on *Older* – I took my first experience of bereavement and tried to take all the most optimistic lessons from it," said George.

The album also produced a slam-bang dance-floor filler in the shape of "Fastlove", another UK Number 1. The song's super-slick video – including a soaking wet George dancing his heart out – was directed by the highly experienced team of Vaughan Arnell and Anthea Benton and won an International Viewer's Choice Award at that year's MTV Video Music Awards.

Change was on the way in George's personal life too – during the making of *Older*, he had started a new relationship: "I feel as though Anselmo sent me Kenny at the exact time that I would need him."

ABOVE George Michael and his partner Kenny Goss at the Versace Couture Collection Fashion Show After Party.

OPPOSITE Filming his dance-floor hit, "Fastlove", in 1996.

"THE KIND OF OPTIMISM I SHOWED ON *OLDER* - I TOOK MY FIRST EXPERIENCE OF BEREAVEMENT AND TRIED TO TAKE ALL THE MOST OPTIMISTIC LESSONS FROM IT"

GEORGE MICHAEL

American businessman Kenny Goss had met George in Los Angeles. They became a couple; no hiding, no lies: "*Everyone* knew," Goss would later say. "We would go to restaurants and hold hands. It's just that he hadn't gone on a television show and said, 'I am a gay man.'"

SUPPORT FROM ELTON

Despite the happiness, George could be forgiven for thinking that the odds were still stacked against him; soon after meeting Goss, George lost his mother to skin cancer in February 1997. The grieving singer missed the Brit Awards that year – he'd won Best Male for the third time – and Elton John accepted the award for his absent friend, reading out a message of thanks and apology on his behalf.

Elton and George would support each other over another tragic passing that year – that of Diana, Princess of Wales. The world had been rocked by the news of her death in a car crash in Paris, along with Dodi Al-Fayed, son of Harrods' owner,

Mohammed Al-Fayed. George had first met the Princess in 1993 after she had asked him to appear at an AIDS fundraising concert. Since then he'd visited her at Buckingham Palace: "She was like a lot of women who have been attracted to me in my life," he later said. "They see something non-threatening. There were certain things that happened that made it very clear that she was very attracted to me."

George and Elton arrived together on the day of Diana's funeral – along with Elton's partner, David Furnish. One of the most moving sections saw Elton perform "Candle In The Wind", barely able to suppress his emotions. Always willing to use a tragic event as an opportunity to give back, George would donate the *Older* track "You Have Been Loved" to a Diana tribute album. The song was released as a single and was kept from the Number 1 slot by Elton's "Candle In The Wind 1997".

OPPOSITE George in the congregation of Princess Diana's funeral on 6 September 1997.

OPPOSITE The singer arriving at the restaurant Spago, after openly admitting he was gay in an interview with CNN on 10 April 1998.

LEFT Reading out a statement at the headquarters of Project Angel Food. Following his arrest, and later charge, with lewd conduct in 1998, George had to carry out 80 hours of community service.

OVERLEAF Stevie Wonder and George Michael team up for a rock duet in 1997.

UNDERCOVER

With his mother's passing, and his very public involvement in the funeral of Diana, Princess of Wales, George later said he felt that the press backed off and left him alone for a while. If that was indeed the case, things would change drastically after an incident at the public toilets at Will Rogers Memorial Park in Beverly Hills; in fact, it would forever change the public's perception of George. 'Something in me said, *You shouldn't go in there, there's something really dodgy going on,*" he would later recall, casting his mind back to the events of 7 April 1998. "But I went in..."

George had just been to lunch and visited the toilets at the park. There he had an encounter with an undercover police officer – moments later he was arrested and later charged with lewd conduct. The press had what they'd desired for years – they were able to "out" George Michael and get the headlines they had always wanted to print: ZIP ME UP BEFORE YOU GO GO was *The Sun*'s contribution. "Running naked up and down Oxford Street singing 'I Am What I Am' would have been a more dignified way of coming out," George admitted.

He received a $810 fine and was ordered to carry out 80 hours of community service – which was carried out under the full glare of the cameras – and became the butt of every comedian on the planet. But George refused to play the tortured, closeted artist. "People say to me, *What were you thinking?* Well, it's nice to make people laugh once in a while... but I also knew that having made a complete fool of myself, I really better come up with a hit song."

Which is exactly what he did. George was often at his most carefree when heading on to the dance floor and the single "Outside" was the perfect glitterball repost to his critics. Featuring samples of BBC news reports about his arrest, a thumping disco beat and a lyric celebrating the joys of al fresco sex, the song was a Number 2 hit in the UK. The accompanying video went even further, with George in full police uniform, gyrating in a futuristic disco-toilet. If the whole incident wasn't surreal enough, the officer involved in the real-life case then tried to sue George for $10 million for the emotional distress being involved in the incident had caused him.

The single acted as a taster for George's Greatest Hits collection released at the end of the year. With perhaps another nod to the place where he'd been arrested, it was called *Ladies & Gentlemen*. "I'll never get arrested again," George said at the time. "It never should have happened. It didn't happen by accident. Am I going to put myself in a public situation like that again? Of course not. Are they going to try and humiliate me again? Very possibly."

LIGHTING THE TOUCH PAPER

Nineteen ninety-nine saw George giving his time and his star power to good causes, worthy projects and people close to his heart. He performed at the Royal Albert Hall at the *Concert For Linda,* held to mark the passing of Linda McCartney, with proceeds going to a range of animal charities. George shared a stage with Tom Jones, Elvis Costello and Paul McCartney himself, along with the event's organizer, Chrissie Hynde. He also returned to his old stomping ground of Wembley Stadium for NetAid, joining the likes of David Bowie, Bryan Adams and Robbie Williams to raise money and awareness for a campaign to cancel Third World debt.

To see out the millennium, George released a covers' album just before Christmas 1999. *Songs*

From The Last Century saw him paired with producer Phil Ramone, the multi-award-winner behind albums by everyone from Burt Bacharach, Aretha Franklin and George's old sparring partner, Frank Sinatra. The album was a mix of old standards and newer songs – such as "Roxanne" by The Police – performed in a jazzy, sophisticated style. The album reached Number 2 in the UK but didn't trouble the *Billboard* Top 100 in America. Creatively, the album may not have stretched him, but George was satisfied with the quality of the end result: "I honestly wanted to stay afloat personally by having something to do... working with Phil Ramone, singing songs that would stretch my voice."

George's generosity was again much in evidence around this time, after he bid nearly £1.5 million to buy John Lennon's piano to stop it going to an overseas buyer. The 1970 Steinway Model Z upright that "Imagine" was written on had previously been housed at The Beatles Story museum in Liverpool.

OPPOSITE George sings at the Pavarotti & Friends concert in Modena, Italy, on 6 June 2006.

ABOVE Tom Jones and George Michael on stage at the tribute concert to Linda McCartney on 10 April 1999.

RIGHT The legendary musician Paul McCartney with Chrissie Hynde, Tom Jones, George Michael, Des'ree, Elvis Costello, Eddie Izzard and Sinéad O'Connor during the Here, There and Everywhere tribute concert.

"I BECAME SO AWARE OF HOW INTRINSIC TO MY ENTIRE BEING IT IS TO CREATE MUSIC. I LOST THE MUSIC THAT WAS AT THE CENTRE OF ME, WHICH WAS LIKE LOSING GOD. IT WAS THE DARKEST TIME"

GEORGE MICHAEL

At the time of the purchase George said it was "worth every penny" and that he'd already decided what he was going to do with it: "Having paid one and a half million pounds for it I'd really like to play something on it and stick it on my next record. So as I'm recording right now, I think I'll hold on to it for a couple of months and see if I can get it on to my new record and then it's going back to the museum in Liverpool where I think it rightly belongs. It's not the type of thing that should be in storage somewhere or being protected; it should be seen by people."

NEW INSPIRATION

George's attempt at recording new material was proving to be a slow and frustrating affair. "I spent a lot of time trying to work, really trying to work," he later said. "Going into the studio day after day after day... pretending that it's not breaking my heart. I became so aware of how intrinsic to my entire being it is to create music. I lost the music that was at the centre of me, which was like losing God. It was the darkest time."

Inspiration would come from an even darker source. George had become increasingly concerned about the way Britain and America were, in his view, fanning the flames of religious fundamentalism overseas, and had started writing a song that expressed his fears. This was brought into sharp relief with the terrorist attacks on the Twin Towers in New York on 11 September 2001: "I was totally freaked out that what I had been writing about was happening in front of my eyes... it was just the worst thing to ever conceive of doing something as evil as that, but I felt confused because I'd written this song for a reason, but know the reason was very puzzling. I certainly didn't want to look opportunistic, so I sat on the song and didn't know what to do with it."

George waited until the summer of 2002 before releasing the song he'd been working on and the single "Shoot The Dog", but it still proved to be as incendiary as he'd feared. Twenty years after the release of the gentle social commentary of "Wham Rap (Enjoy What You Do!)", he went all out to share his views on George W. Bush, Tony Blair and the situation in the Middle East.

OPPOSITE George Michael with Welsh singer Charlotte Church.

ABOVE The singer performs on stage at 'NetAiD' in Wembley Stadium, on 9 October 1999.

Just to ram the point home, the single was accompanied by a cartoon video produced by the team behind the British TV satire show *2DTV*. The video featured a scattergun blast of political and pop culture references – from Phil Oakey of The Human League (the song features a Human League sample) to Cherie Blair, the Village People, David Beckham and the anti-war movie *Dr. Strangelove*.

Prior to its release, George ignored the usual promotional opportunities and instead did the rounds of heavyweight political and current affairs shows. He warned Sir David Frost that "we are about to light the touch paper of all these

pockets of Islamic fundamentalism by doing something that's completely illegal."

The press licked their lips at yet another opportunity to lambast George – the roasting he took made the LA toilet incident look like they'd gone easy on him by comparison. "Has George Michael Lost The Plot, Or Just His Career?" asked the *Daily Mail*. "Pop Perv's 9/11 Slur" mocked the *New York Post*. "People are looking at the song in context of an attack on America," he said, trying to defend his position. "And really, my attack is that Tony Blair is not involving the British in this issue. He's perfectly happy staying up to watch the World Cup and enjoying the Jubilee, all things I'm perfectly guilty of, but there's a serious discussion about Iraq which hasn't taken place. We don't know what Saddam Hussein is capable of, the British public has no idea."

OPPOSITE Geril Halliwell and George at the White Tie and Tiara Ball held at Elton John's Windsor mansion on 5 July 2001.
ABOVE Elizabeth Hurley and George are filmed in the audience for a Versace show at the Théâtre National de Chaillot at the Trocadero in Paris on 8 July 2002.

"I'M NOT PRETENDING I WON'T BE FAMOUS ANY MORE, BUT IN THE MODERN WORLD IF YOU TAKE YOURSELF OUT OF THE FINANCIAL ASPECT OF THINGS, YOU'RE NOT MAKING ANYBODY ANY MONEY, YOU'RE NOT LOSING ANYBODY ANY MONEY."

GEORGE MICHAEL

RIGHT The NetAid press conference at the Landmark Hotel in London, 1999.

OVERLEAF Celebrities including George Michael, Julie Walters, Sue Cook, Sade, Danniella Westbrook and Jenni Falconer attend the appeal press launch for The Rainbow Trust in the Meridien Hotel, London, on 18 September 2003.

The British public decided that they were perfectly capable of making up their own minds about "Shoot The Dog" and the song was a reasonable hit, getting to Number 12 in the UK charts. But George was bruised by the mauling he'd received: "[Rupert] Murdoch was getting his way. That was massively depressing to me. I got a kicking from Rupert Murdoch, I got a bunch of homophobia that was reserved for me since I'd 'escaped' the clutches of the press in LA, and it floored me. It was ironic that the first thing ever that floored me from the press was nothing to do with my private life."

PATIENCE

The album the song featured on was the ironically entitled *Patience*. "I know this will sound arrogant, but I know when I'm good," he said about his fans' lengthy wait for the album. "And I know when I'm not. Which is why everything took so long."

Demonstrating that it was always difficult to second-guess him, George had returned to Sony to release *Patience*. He also warned that anyone expecting another album – at least, one that adhered to the traditional record industry format – would have a very long wait indeed. He'd had enough of the industry and any future releases would be offered online in exchange for a donation. "I'm sure it's unprecedented," he said. "It's definitely unprecedented for someone who still sells records. I've been very well remunerated for my talents over the years, so I really don't need the public's money. It takes the pressure off to have a collection of songs every so many years, which is what nearly killed me. I'm not pretending I won't be famous any more, but in the modern world if you take yourself out of the financial aspect of things, you're not making anybody any money, you're not losing anybody any money. Believe me, I'll be of very little interest to the press in a certain number of years."

ABOVE George Michael on *Breakfast with Frost* in 2003.
RIGHT Appearing at the Virgin Megastore, Los Angeles, to publicize the release of his new album *Patience*.

JUST
WHO I AM

As if tidying up loose ends at the end of an era, George took part in a documentary called *A Different Story* in 2004. What started as a "fly-on-the-wall" piece soon settled down into a fairly traditional "talking heads" style music documentary. It's believed that George, unhappy with the way the film was going, bought the footage and finished the film himself. The finished documentary saw the singer reunited with Andrew Ridgeley – the pair were interviewed together, though they clearly found it difficult to maintain a sense of seriousness when in each other's company. Ridgeley had virtually disappeared from the public eye by this time and was living the quiet life in Cornwall with his partner Keren Woodward of Bananarama. "Do I think I've missed out my not pursuing music as a lifelong career?" Ridgeley said. "May have." George disagreed, believing that his old

friend had it good – he seemed jealous of Ridgeley and the low-key life he had made for himself.

Ridgeley's relative anonymity must have seemed even more attractive to George in 2006 after a series of incidents that put him back in the spotlight – but not for his music. In February he was arrested on suspicion of possessing drugs after being found slumped at the wheel of his car at Hyde Park Corner in London. It was, he said, "my own stupid fault, as usual." Two months later it was claimed he'd driven off after hitting three parked cars in an incident in north London. In July he was snapped by the *News Of The World* in an area of Hampstead Heath known as a cruising area for gay men. Once again, George was cast as the "troubled star" but came out fighting – defending himself in a series of interviews, even appearing live on ITN News: "I do not deserve the criticism," he stated angrily. "What I don't have respect for is some demand for answers from an openly gay man who is living his own life. I have not cheated or lied about my sex life to anybody in my life, in my entire life. I hate not to be able to rise above it, but there is only so much you can take."

ABOVE George Michael attends court in 2006 pleading guilty to the charge of driving while unfit through drugs.

OPPOSITE The artist performs at the BankAtlantic Center in Sunrise, Florida, on 3 August 2008.

Rumours and lurid headlines swirled around him – a planned wedding to Kenny Goss had been cancelled, the papers said; his record company were demanding that he "curb his sex and drugs wild ways"; his friend Elton John wanted friends to intervene and help George but the singer was having none of it: "Elton just needs to shut his mouth and get on with his own life. Look, if people choose to believe that I'm sitting here in my ivory tower, Howard Hughesing myself with long fingernails and loads of drugs, then I can't do anything about that, can I? People want to see me as tragic with all the cottaging and drug-taking… those things are not what most people aspire to, and I think it removes people's envy to see your weaknesses. I don't even see them as weaknesses any more. It's just who I am."

25 LIVE TOUR

The best answer to his critics came in the form of his 25 Live Tour – the greatest hits live package that started in Barcelona in September 2006, snaking its way across more than 40 countries, expanding continually as it went. Along the way he christened the new Wembley Stadium – who else could

they ask? – and earned himself in the region of £50 million for the tour as a whole. During the run of shows he was believed to have received more than £1.5 million for one night's work singing a 13-song New Year's set for Russian billionaire Vladimir Potanin. His coffers were bolstered even further with a greatest hits album that featured tracks from Wham!'s *Fantastic* right up to newer songs like "Flawless (Go To The City)" and "This Is Not Real Love".

However, this being George Michael, the success was tempered by lurid headlines about his lifestyle – in 2007 he pleaded guilty to driving while unfit under the influence of drugs after police found his car obstructing traffic lights in Cricklewood, north-west London. "I did something very stupid and I am very ashamed since doing it," he told the judge. "I'm not used to defending myself in a position where I am ashamed of something."

BELOW Performing at a concert in Amsterdam, on 26 June 2007.

OPPOSITE George Michael at the 25 Live Tour Opener in Barcelona, 2006.

OVERLEAF The artist performs on stage in Bratislava, 25 May 2007, during his European tour.

George showed he wasn't adverse to sending himself up as a way of dealing with the negative attention – he played himself in the 2007 Christmas Special episode of the Ricky Gervais comedy series *Extras*, cruising for sex on his lunch break from community service. But in 2008 he was in trouble with the law again, this time for possession of drugs after being arrested in a toilet in Hampstead Heath. The upmarket London enclave would also be the setting for the incident that would finally be a slip-up too far for George. In July 2010 he crashed his car into a Snappy Snaps photo developing shop on Hampstead High Street. The singer was later found guilty of driving while unfit through drugs and sentenced to eight weeks in prison. He served four weeks – largely at HM Prison Highpoint South in Suffolk – but carried out the first part of his sentence at the notoriously tough HM Prison Pentonville. It was literally a sobering experience: "Pentonville was really quite horrific and I was put in with the paedophiles and the

bullies," he later revealed. "I didn't leave my cell very much in those few days. It shook me out of my denial in a way that the others hadn't... So from the day after that crash happened, I started in drug counselling."

This period of change in George's life coincided with his split from Kenny Goss: "He's brought me a lot of joy and a lot of pain and I'm so sorry things have not worked out," he later said. "I'm so sad about my relationship with Kenny."

OPPOSITE George leaving Highbury Corner Magistrates' Court, London, surrounded by press and police on 24 August 2010. He pleaded guilty to driving under the influence of drugs and possessing cannabis after he crashed his car into a photo processing shop in London on 4 July 2010.

ABOVE British comedian Ricky Gervais and George in the pressroom at the GQ Men Of The Year Awards at the Royal Opera House, London, on 7 September 2004.

OVERLEAF George Michael walks along a catwalk among his audience during his 25 Live Tour at Wembley Stadium, London, on 9 June 2007.

LAST HURRAH

George threw himself into a wide range of projects – he released a cover version of New Order's "True Faith" for Comic Relief as well as performing a sketch with comic actor James Corden, where the pair made the prototype for Corden's wildly popular "Carpool Karaoke" series. He proved himself highly adept as a comedian, sulking because he wasn't allowed to go to Comic Relief: "You're a joke, George," exclaimed Corden. "I can't walk into Comic Relief with you – Comic Relief is about helping people like you!"

The idea of Corden singing in a car with a guest celeb would become a key part of the actor's success in the US, with everyone from Mariah Carey to First Lady Michelle Obama taking part. "It was the first time I'd ever sung in a car with anybody," Corden would later recall. "It's become quite a big part of my life now, and he [George] really inspired it. When we started the [*Late Late*] show here, we were trying to get people to do 'Carpool Karaoke', and not many artists wanted to do it. We would send them this clip of me and George, and we went to Mariah Carey, and she was the first person to say yes. Her words were, 'If it's good enough for George, then it's good enough for me. I'll do it.' So, we all have so much to thank him for, for the music that he's given that will last for ever. But we personally, here at this show, we owe him so much."

But George's last great creative hurrah would come in a series of performances on a very much grander scale than two men singing in a car. The Symphonica Tour would criss-cross Europe for more than a year, with a set of songs largely pulled from the more reflective side of his back catalogue, performed with a full orchestra.

LEFT George Michael performs during a special gala charity concert in aid of French AIDS charity Sidaction, as part of his Symphonica Tour at Palais Garnier, Paris, on 9 September 2012.

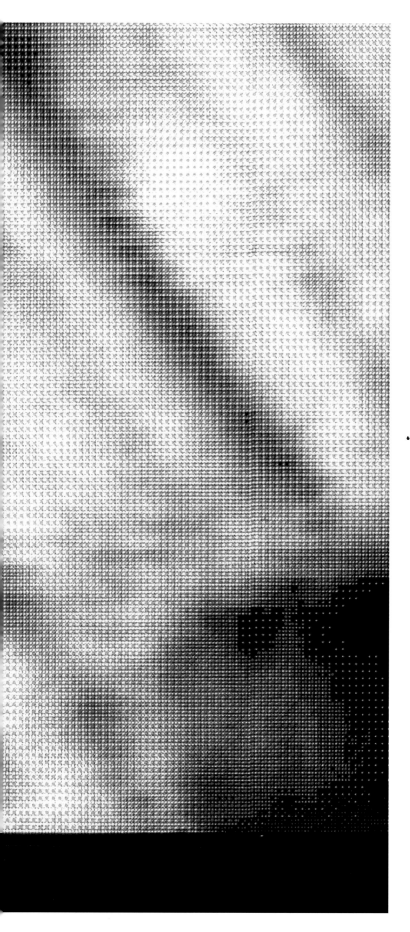

The opening night at the State Opera House in Prague in August 2011 garnered a rave review from *The Guardian* newspaper: "The whole evening is packed with songs of emotional heft and resonance, lovingly interpreted," it said. "After violins underscore the elegant angst of 'A Different Corner', Michael constructs an upbeat climax to the set with a soulful roustabout through Nina Simone's celebratory anthem 'Feeling Good' then encores with Stevie Wonder's 'You and I' and a medley of his own life-affirming dance-pop hits in 'Amazing', Wham's 'I'm Your Man' and 'Freedom', his five-minute standing ovation is entirely deserved."

An album to accompany the tour was later released and became his seventh Number 1 in the UK. Despite everything, George Michael was back at the top of his game.

"SO, WE ALL HAVE SO MUCH TO THANK HIM FOR, FOR THE MUSIC THAT HE'S GIVEN THAT WILL LAST FOR EVER"

JAMES CORDEN

LEFT George Michael performs at Etihad Stadium, Melbourne, on 3 March 2010.
OVERLEAF The announcement of George's 2011 Symphonica Tour was made at the Royal Opera House, London, on 11 May 2011.

MY BELOVED FRIEND

"I do believe that I'm a lot better singer now than I ever thought I'd be," was George's view when asked to assess his career around this time. As for the future: "I want to leave something as a writer and think to have a passion, to have something that drives you on through life in a creative sense, most of us want to leave something, want to have something that will be remembered without people really having to search in their memory. And I want to leave songs; if I can leave songs that will mean something to other generations."

George was by now in a relationship with London-based Australian hairdresser to the stars Fadi Fawaz and his Symphonica Tour was continuing across Europe to sell-out crowds and rave reviews. But in October 2011 he pulled out of a planned performance at London's Royal Albert Hall due to a viral infection – a few days later he was deemed well enough to continue to perform in Vienna but was again hospitalized hours before he was to take to the stage. Rumours began to swirl

about the true nature of his illness – doctors at the Vienna hospital said that George was suffering from pneumonia and had been in intensive care. "They spent three weeks keeping me alive," he said after being finally released from hospital in the run-up to Christmas. "It was, by far, the worst month of my life. The hospital they rushed me to was absolutely the best place in the world I could have been to deal with pneumonia. I have to believe that someone thinks I've still got some work to do here."

He was well enough in the New Year to make an unexpected appearance at the Brit Awards to present Adele with her gong for Best Album. "I found him to be one of the truest icons, because a lot of the time, with people who are that globally known and famous, there tends to be... not a fakeness in a bad way, but they put on this massive bravado and alter-ego to protect themselves," Adele would later say. "And he was very British. No matter where his career or love life took him, he always remained true to Britain and they gave him a hard time a lot of the time, but he still stayed loyal until the very end. I relate to that – no matter how much I try to escape Britain sometimes, my roots are there. I took great comfort in him."

ABOVE With his partner, Fadi Fawaz.

OPPOSITE Moody pictures of George attending a press conference at the Royal Opera House in London, 2011.

THE WORLD STAGE

After making a full recovery, George was back on the world stage later that year for the Closing Ceremony of the Olympic Games in London. The Games had been a roaring success but George faced a barrage of criticism for his contribution. After a rousing "Freedom! '90" he launched into a new song, a low-key house track called "White Light", which he'd written after his near-death experience in Vienna. Many were angry that he seemed to use the occasion to promote a new song rather than simply entertain the crowd and the global TV audience with his hits. As ever, he was unrepentant: "I hope you are not bothered by the press reports of my scandalous 'promotion'!!!" he tweeted. "It was my one chance on TV to thank you all for your loyalty and prayers, and I took it. And I don't regret it."

The press would have their final chance to splash his personal life across their pages the following year. George had somehow managed to fall from his car onto the M1 near St Albans – he'd been in the back of the chauffeur-driven vehicle and was apparently trying to close the passenger door after discovering that it wasn't shut properly. He was airlifted to hospital and treated for cuts and bruises – he then had to fend off claims that he'd thrown himself from the vehicle on purpose.

Drama, it seemed, was never far away when it came to George Michael. He was "shutting himself away because of a mystery illness" by the summer of 2014, according to some press reports. Literally the next day he was supposedly hinting at a Wham! reunion, reuniting to play Glastonbury. Then he was staying in a Swiss rehab clinic; next he was addicted to crack cocaine. With no proper evidence to fill their pages, the press went with speculation and rumour.

OPPOSITE Adele accepting the Best Album Award from George at the Brit Awards in 2012.

ABOVE George in Paris at Palais Garnier on 9 September 2012.

OVERLEAF Singing "Freedom! '90" and "White Light", George was one of the acts to take part in the Closing Ceremony of the London Olympics, 2012.

"I DO BELIEVE THAT I'M A LOT BETTER SINGER NOW THAN I EVER THOUGHT I'D BE"

GEORGE MICHAEL

FREEDOM

Finally, in 2015, some real news: a new documentary and a re-release of a classic album. A message was posted on George's official social-media accounts stating: "George Michael is busy putting the finishing touches to his special documentary film *Freedom*. He has discovered some incredible, unseen archive footage and is shooting additional interviews for the project, so the film will now air in March 2017. It promises to be a real treat for fans! To coincide with the film's broadcast, George and Sony Music have decided to move the reissue of the *Listen Without Prejudice* album to the same time."

Looking to the past was one thing, but it soon became apparent that fans had something to look forward to that represented the future too. Shahid Khan – otherwise known as British songwriter and producer Naughty Boy, who'd found fame working with Emeli Sandé and Sam Smith – told the BBC that people could expect new music from George in 2017 and that the pair would be working together: "I can't wait," said Khan. "I don't know what to expect. And, to be honest, he's more mysterious than anyone else so I'm actually excited. I reached out and then he got back. He's got an album coming out next year, and he's going to be doing something for my album as well."

OPPOSITE AND BELOW The artist at the Closing Ceremony of the London Olympics, 2012.

TRAGEDY

Less than two weeks later, on Christmas Day 2016, George was found dead at his home in Goring-on-Thames, Oxfordshire. He was 53. A statement was released at 11 p.m. that evening by his publicist, Michael Lippman, which said: "It is with great sadness that we can confirm our beloved son, brother and friend George passed away peacefully at home over the Christmas period. The family would ask that their privacy be respected at this difficult and emotional time. There will be no further comment at this stage."

George's house in Goring-on-Thames became a mini-shrine, with locals leaving flowers. Those tributes were soon swelled by fans who travelled out to the quiet village to pay their respects. The singer's other residence in Highgate – The Grove – became the main focus for those wishing to pay their respects, with cards, flowers, toys and even Cypriot flags being left at the site. George's Land Rover car was covered in lipstick messages and even the Snappy Snaps shop that he'd crashed into became a magnet for fans.

George's famous friends paid their own tributes: "I am in deep shock," said Sir Elton John. "I have lost a beloved friend – the kindest, most generous soul and a brilliant artist. My heart goes out to his family and all of his fans."

Madonna, reflecting the feelings of many after the deaths of David Bowie and Prince earlier that year, said: "Farewell my friend! Another great artist leaves us."

But perhaps the most moving words came from the man who knew George better than anyone. The man who, as a child, had stuck up his hand at Bushey Meads School in 1975 to volunteer to look after the "new kid".

"Heartbroken at the loss of my beloved friend Yog," said Andrew Ridgeley. "Me, his loved ones, his friends, the world of music, the world at large. 4ever loved. A xx".

RIGHT AND OVERLEAF Tributes of flowers, letters, photographs and candles left outside the house of pop music icon George Michael.

"I WANT TO LEAVE SOMETHING AS A WRITER AND THINK TO HAVE A PASSION, TO HAVE SOMETHING THAT DRIVES YOU ON THROUGH LIFE IN A CREATIVE SENSE, MOST OF US WANT TO LEAVE SOMETHING, WANT TO HAVE SOMETHING THAT WILL BE REMEMBERED WITHOUT PEOPLE HAVING TO SEARCH IN THEIR MEMORY"

GEORGE MICHAEL

FAITH RESTORED

The very newspapers that knew they had a front-page lead every time George Michael made a mistake when he was alive painted a very different picture of him immediately after his death.

Newspapers that had written disparagingly abut his weight, his lifestyle, his politics and his sexuality began singing from a very different hymn sheet after we lost him. George was "pop royalty", they said... a "music legend"... an "international pop sensation".

Then, those same papers reported another, very different, very secret side to the singer – his extraordinary generosity. Stories began to emerge, often from people who'd been sworn to secrecy while George was alive. He'd donated millions to the kids' charity Childline, including royalties from his single "Jesus To A Child"; he regularly gave free tickets to his shows to NHS workers, and even tipped one student nurse £5,000 while she was working as a waitress to make ends meet; he'd spotted a contestant on a TV quiz show saying he and his wife needed money for IVF treatment – George had phoned the producers and given them £15,000. The beneficiary – Lynette Gillard from Bolton – never knew who had given them the money. "For many years I wondered who would have been so generous and now I know," she said when the donor's identity was finally revealed. "What more can I say other than, 'Thank you, George'?"

At the time of the mystery donation in 2008, her partner, Steve Davies, said: "Thank you is not enough. It restores your faith in humankind. All the bad news you read about and then something like this happens."

As well as this slightly dazed sense of not fully appreciating the kind of person that George Michael was until after his death, there was also a reappraisal of his achievements. The singer, performer and producer was, lest we forget, the man who'd

OPPOSITE AND OVERLEAF The singer-songwriter on his Faith World Tour.

co-written "Careless Whisper" when he was 17; he'd steered his way through fashions and fads to stay on top of the most fickle of businesses for the best part of 35 years; and he'd taken on a global business entity like Sony when he felt he wasn't being respected as an artist.

Despite those who sniffed that he'd done much of this while hiding his true identity and sexuality, George Michael believed that, above all else, he'd stayed true to himself: "I never wanted to be someone else," he once said. "I wanted to be a star and for people to love me and recognize me in the street – as a child that's what I really wanted – but I never wanted to be someone else. I think that the people that are the most vivid, colourful, fascinating stars are basically people who want to be someone else. I believe that of Madonna, I believe that of Prince, I believe that of Michael Jackson. I'm not saying it's a terrible flaw; it actually makes them very, very interesting people. But I've never seen myself in that light."

From the denim-clad kid grabbing that first opportunity to appear on *Top of the Pops* with both hands, to the respected artist inspiring the likes of Adele and Sam Smith, George Michael has left a legacy of music, fashion and memories to last several lifetimes. We won't see his like again.

But how did *he* want to be remembered? How did he view his legacy? "I don't believe that I am important as a pop star, I don't think that there are many people that are important as pop stars in the sense that they used to be," he once said. "I don't believe I will leave a great mark as an entity. I think I'm more realistic than that. I don't feel that need to prove anything, that I'm a different kind of person. Which leaves me open to pursue the second thought, which is I would like to leave something special behind me, which is nothing really to do with me as a person being [in] any way different, just my abilities as a songwriter. It's my songs I think I can concentrate on now."